# TABLE OF CONTENTS

# TABLE OF CONTENTS

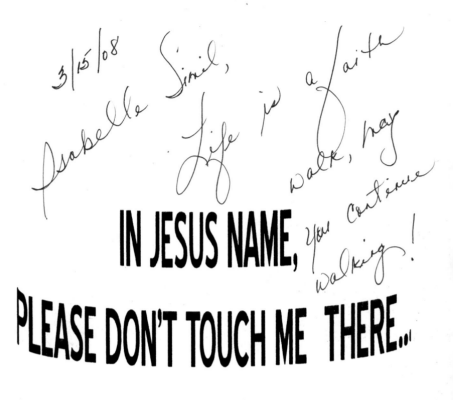

3/15/08

Isabelle Siniel,

Life is a faith walk, may you continue walking!

# IN JESUS NAME,

# PLEASE DON'T TOUCH ME THERE...

**Mitzi L. Carrasquillo**
a u t h o r

God Bless,

Mitzi . Carrasquillo

ISBN 978-0-9799006-2-4

Additional copies of this book may be obtained by writing, phone, email or by visiting the website at www.favortwou.net

Publisher Favortwou, Incorporated
404.228.0316 ~ 404.428.1179
Favortwou@hotmail.com

Printed in the United States by
Morris Publishing
3212 E. Hwy. 30
Kearney, NE 68847

Cover designed by: Nicholas Peterson ~ Atlanta, GA

Author Photographed by: Maya Darasaw (Celebrity Kids Portrait Studios)

# $=$ P R E FA C E $=$

## Your Life IS Worthwhile

November 9, 1993 my father left a Suicide Note, his body has never been found.

Eight years later the suicide seed he planted was about to manifest in his only daughter.......

# DEDICATION

$\mathbf{F}$ather in the name of Jesus, I pray this book will inspire and motivate every person suffering from depression, sexual abuse and rape. May it Love, Heal, and Restore all that read it.

*…"And the peace of God, which surpasses all understanding,*
*will guard your hearts and minds*
*through Christ Jesus"…*
**(Philippians 4:7)**

In Jesus **N**ame
*Amen*

# ACKNOWLEDGEMENT

Thank you first and foremost to my Lord and Savior Jesus Christ, there would be no *"In Jesus Name, Please Don't Touch Me There"* without you. **Thank you for your Mercy and Grace that kept me, I am truly honored to carry out your assignment.**

To my husband, best friend, and biggest supporter, thank you for allowing me to do this book. I Praise God for your encouragement, never ending patience and understanding! Even when you didn't know what to say, you said it just by listening, and being there. Your comfort and support helped more than you could imagine. Not to mention the numerous Dunkin Donuts runs for coffee, but most of all your presence. I love you!

To my beautiful children, Jeanee, Jazmine, and Jose thank you for your Prayers, hugs, kisses, and keeping quiet when needed. My greatest joy comes from watching you grow and serve and in the Lord. Mommy loves you!

**A special thank you to Jazmine, I am enormously grateful for your poem, cover inspiration, and most of all your strength.**

To my parents, Jesse and Jean Spencer-Hodges, I Love You Dearly! Sometimes we as parents, carry this sense of guilt as if we should of, would of, or could have done more. This is a normal feeling to have, but always remember that you did what you could do with what you had at the time. And I am thankful to be Blessed with parents as you.

Much love to my brothers Reginald, Lorenzo, Marcus, and Damien, Sisters Krystal and Dionne, we are Mom's Special Seven.

I know we have seven different testimonies and some may not be so special, but having siblings as you, is very special to me. I love you.

Grandma Spencer, You understood me when I didn't understand myself, you made sense of things even when they made no sense to me. If needed, you would even slap the sense into me, literally.

Thank you for always Praying and being there for me. I now understand why every question that I asked you was given a Biblical answer...

*I Love You First...*
Your, Eldest Granddaughter


Thank you Jesus for my Spiritual Parents, Dwayne and Kitt Brewington!

I've visited and attended numerous churches, I was a church hopper. Never stayed in any one too long, was always running, looking for something. Some churches I never gave a chance, some I judged by the distance, some by how much gas I had in the car, etc. I made many excuses for attending or not attending.

Praise God for placing my family at your "home" that beautiful Father's Day, June 8, 2001!

Pastor Brew and Kitt, there are not enough words to thank you for snapping me in the high chair, tying my bib, airplane the food in my mouth while feeding me. Even sometimes when I drooled, letting some slip out or forgot to swallow, you were right there to push it back in and daring me not to swallow, drool, or spit up again...

You are a living example of the calling of a Man and Woman of God.

Thank you for allowing me to be one of your sheep.

*"...Then I will give you shepherds after my own heart,*
*who will lead you with knowledge*
*and understanding..."*
**(Jeremiah 3:15)**

---

*Many special thanks to all of my Angels,*

Father Coyne *(St. Angela's Catholic Church)*, Mattapan, Massachusetts, Ms. Lorraine and Deanna Woodbury, Dr. Creflo and Taffi Dollar *(World Changers Church International)* College Park, Georgia, Jeannette K. Reynoso, Patricia McGee,Minister Roosevelt Doctor and First Lady Minnie *(The House of Our Lord)* Dorchester, Massachusetts, Kenneth and Gloria Copeland Ministries *(Eagle Mountain International Church)*, Fort Worth, Texas, Jerry Savelle Ministries International, Crowley, Texas, The Hill-McGee Family, Douglas Davis Jr., Joan M. Davis, and the entire Davis Family, The Green Family, The Greene Family, The Spencer Family, Hortencia Lopez-Carrasquillo, Gracias mucho para el regalo de su hijo lindo, The Carrasquillo Family, The Cintron Family, Diana, the word "in-law" does not exist in our relationship, thank you for being my "Sister". The Ortiz Family, The Reynoso Family, The Alston Family, Eddie and Vera Doctor, James T. Garrett, Diane Rascoe-Staples, Carol Young, Dee Borden, Cathy Yvette Perry, Gloria Michelle Houston, Katrina Rawles, Veronica Robinson, Aida Reynoso, Monica Costa, Regina Frazier, Fannie Young, Elder Tammie Grice, My Boston University *Family*, Mary Guillermo, Mary Beth Dillon, Susan Janssen, Kathy Sirios, and Joseph "Ole Man Joe" Pascarella, My beautiful Hair Stylist, Donna Cline-Smythe *(Blessed Hands Hair Salon)*, Make-Up Artist, Rebecca Rosales Castillo *(facebyface2002@yahoo)*,

Photographer, Maya Darasaw *(Celebrity Kids Portrait Studios),* Graphic Artist, Nicholas Peterson, it's amazing what you captured in a 15 minute phone call, thank you for the cover! My Publisher and "Maternity Coach" Fay Alice Walker, thank you for your unspeakable patience, faithfulness, and assistance, The entire FavorTwoU, Inc. Publishing Company staff, Alexander Brewington, for sharing your parents with me, My VCCI family, and _____ (place your name here) who has touched my life.

# TESTIMONY

*I have to be a driving force out of darkness into the incredible light...*

*February 26, 2007 - 4:55 a.m.*

Back in the 1970's I remember one of the favorite things to play with whenever I visited my Uncle Doug's house was his living room light switch. Yes, a light switch! It wasn't the regular, boring one that you flipped on the wall or a table lamp's knob that you turned.

In his living room was the type of wall light that *you could control*. I can still remember playing with that knob every time I went to visit. I would stand there and turn it back and forth, dark to light, dim to bright, over and over again. I don't know if it was the fact of having that control or that he had this cooler, newer light fixture in his apartment that we didn't have.

Whenever you turned the knob towards the right the room would get dark, and it would darken as you turned it, then to the left the room would get bright, and brightened as you turned it. As a child, I loved having that ability to control how I wanted the room lit, even if the adults were yelling at me to leave it alone, ("...*you don't pay any light bills around here!...*")

In the same manner that's what depression is, you can decide whether to stay in the dark or make the decision to come out into the light. All of us have the ***ability*** to control whether to live in the dark, or not. We just have to want to do it, or shall I say recognize that we ***need to do it***.

On April 7, 2001, I made the decision to come out of darkness, I turned the light switch to the left, and have refused to play with it, not to the right, not back and forth, not dim to bright, and back again. Just leave it to the left all the way. My decision to keep the light bright was through the Word of God, I could not have done it without HIM.

"...*But you are a chosen generation, a royal priesthood,*
*a holy nation. His own special people,*
*that you may proclaim the praises of*
*Him who called you out of darkness*
*into His marvelous light;...*"
**(1 Peter 2:9)**

# ═══ THE BEGINNING ═══

That was the day that I was sitting in my bedroom closet curled up contemplating how to kill myself. The day that I thought my life was not worthwhile, no reason to live, useless, just a waste.

I was severely depressed, and felt I had no reason to live another day, I didn't want to live another day. I just wanted out, that was my solution. Never mind my husband, three beautiful children, parents, siblings; it was all about me getting out of this darkness.

The plan had to be quick, easy (if there is such a thing) and painless, pills, slit wrist and shooting myself were out of the question. I had to have an assured plan that it would work, and me not knowing how to swim was a definite assurance.

The quick, easy and painless plan was to drive my 1991 Toyota Corolla off the Tobin Bridge in Massachusetts.

But as I sat in the closet with my knees under my chin, crying quietly (because my children were in the next room) to myself, I said three little words in between my sobs, "LORD HELP ME".

After I said those three little words I said nothing else, stayed silent, then I heard something, something familiar, this… this voice…

this voice that I usually always heard over my girlfriend Jeannette's house when she was doing my hair. I like hearing this voice He was so good, was easy to explain and tell a story where I could understand it, it wasn't over my head. His voice was so familiar because he had a strong southern accent; an accent that when he opened his mouth you knew he was from the south!

I was so absorbed in my plan, that I did not realize my TV was on!

His name was funny too, I always wondered if it was his real name though. Well, he was in the middle of telling his story about when he was depressed and wanting to end his life. He went on to say I do not know who this is for....

I crawled out of the closet, kneeled at the side of my bed, laid my head down faced towards the TV and just listened with tears rolling down my face...

As I was so into listening to him, I did not hear the phone ringing. I answered it, still with my face turned to the TV and head on the bed, still on my knees, by the side of the bed. It was my girlfriend Jeannette Reynoso on the phone, and she asked what was I doing, trying to act like I wasn't crying so she couldn't hear it in my voice, she went on to tell me why she called, she had been praying in the Holy Spirit and the Holy Spirit told her to call me because I was contemplating suicide.

I lied of course when she asked me, and tried to continue holding a conversation with her. I told her I was watching that man Creflo Dollar, and she was like oh, ok, but she knew....

Later that evening another friend Patricia McGee called and invited me to her church. I had attended her Church, The House of Our Lord, a few times, I actually enjoyed it. So I told her yes, she asked if I wanted to meet her, I said no and promised her that I would be there.

The next day a new life began for me. I was too afraid to drive my car; I took a taxi with my three kids. At the service I could not wait for the part when they asked people to come to the altar to accept Jesus as their Lord and Savior. I was sitting in the last row (I always sat in the last row) saying to myself I am going up when they do the call this time, usually I always sat on the back row to hide and make a quick exit, not this time.

Benediction is usually at the end, but Minister Roosevelt Doctor said that the Holy Spirit was telling him to go in another direction, so before he started in the Word he gave an altar call, I had never jumped out of my seat so fast, that I tripped over the strap of my pocketbook, and the last $7.00 that I had to get home was stolen, but I did not care!

# MITZI L CARRASQUILLO

No one knew that just hours before I was contemplating taking my life, going straight to Hell.

After many, many years of running, I gave my life to Christ, April 8, 2001.

I never felt pretty as a little girl, I always thought I was ugly. Although my mom made sure that I was dressed nicely and had my hair combed (hot combed).

I still did not feel or look like I was a pretty girl. All through my childhood and teen years I felt dirty, used, invaluable, which I carried into my adult years. Growing up in poverty added to the bonus of worthlessness.

It seems that I was in pain for so many years I became numb to it. Usually I would say that I had a high tolerance for pain, regardless of what kind of pain, I've had everything under the sun happen to me and there is nothing else that can hurt me.

I grew up on welfare, in a domestic abused household, was sexually abused as a child, raped as a teenager, and contemplated suicide as an adult.

I share my testimony to show others that you are not alone

# In Jesus Name, Please Don't Touch Me There

(*I use to think that*), and can overcome anything with the Word of God.

My parents were both raised in Chicago. I was born in the Robert Taylor Homes, South Side Projects of Chicago.

At the age of 4, my parents separated. My mom took my two older brothers and me and moved to Dorchester, Massachusetts, the inner city of Boston.

> "...Brothers, I do not consider myself yet to
> have taken hold of it. But one thing that I do;
> forgetting what is behind and straining toward
> what is ahead, I press on toward the goal
> to win the prize for which God
> called me heavenward
> in Christ Jesus..."
> **(Phil 3:13-14)**

We can't explain it, but whenever we meet someone who it has happened to, they usually don't even have to tell us, we already know.

We are all connected in some strange way; we all have that one thing that connects us. It's a silence that goes over us when we hear it has happened again, whether on the news, to our relatives, people we know or don't know.

The sexual abuse started at the age of 6, and continued until I

# MITZI L CARRASQUILLO

was 16 years old.

As if being abused wasn't enough, it was never a stranger.

I know we have always been taught about the stranger, boogeyman, neighbor across or down the street, school bus driver, etc…

Those who abused me were five trusted relatives and friends, people that my mother would never suspect. Trusted relatives and friends that babysat for me, visited or lived with us. They took away my innocence of playing tackle football in the house and instilled me with such fear that caused me to sleep at night with my pajama top and bottom safety pinned together or curled in a ball at bedtime in my blanket so tight that it was hard breathing at night.

As a child you are always taught to respect, trust, and obey "grown people". But what do you do when "grown people" do sexual things to you? Do you obey them when they tell you not to tell anyone or do you obey your mom when she tells you not to disrespect "grown people" and do as they say?

And when you tell your mom and she doesn't believe you, how do you feel? When the abusers say that you are lying and you get a whopping, how do you feel? Sometimes I felt like "Little Red Riding

Hood", like I was always crying wolf…

I use to feel like I had no where to go and no one to turn to. I had very low self esteem and no value of self worth, and always felt that it was my fault.

> "….*For everyone born of God overcomes*
> *the world. This is the victory that*
> *has overcome the world,*
> *even our faith….*"
> **(1John 5:4)**

Everyone's life has a purpose; God has many plans for you…

> "…*For I know the plans I have for you,*
> *declares the Lord, plans to give*
> *you hope and a future…*"
> **(Jeremiah 29:11)**

I know what I am doing. I have it all planned-out plans to take care of you, not abandon, plans to give you the future you hope for.

The Message Bible

For I know the thoughts and plans that I have for you says the Lord, thoughts and plans for welfare and peace and not for evil, to give you hope in your final outcome.

The Amplified Bible

It took me years to receive or believe any of those scriptures, regardless which Bible translation they were in.

This scripture was one that has always been said to me as far back as age 12 when we attended St. Angela's Church in Mattapan, Mass; Father Coyne would pat me on the head as I left Sunday school and say this scripture to me.

Because of what I experienced in my younger years, I did not care about knowing or hearing this scripture.

I think I cared more about him messing up my hair than, hearing his "every Sunday as I left Sunday school scripture".

Around the age of 14 or 15 we would have "study" at home with a brother or sister from the Kingdom Hall, and for some "strange reason" they would say this scripture also.

I never paid mind to it, or even care what it meant. I just knew that every time I turned around someone was in my face quoting it. So I started seeing it as a generic scripture that every religious person said. It used to get on my last nerves!

Sometimes I would be at the mall and a sister would approach me to minister, and here comes the scripture, I would over talk her so ignorantly and say yeah, yeah, yeah I know God has many plans for you blah, blah, blah, here we go again…

Was that the only scripture that they knew? Was it the first one that they taught them? Was it a cult? Did they all have to learn this as a training scripture? All I know was that it was always being said to me and got on my nerves, whether at the mall, or on the street.

> *"…In this is love, not that we loved God, but that He loved us and sent His Son (Jesus Christ) to be a sacrifice for our sins…"*
> **(I John 4:10)**

*Whose plan was this?*

I was raped in my bedroom at the age of 14, and I lived with the fear of Mom finding out since the day it happened…

My Mom said; *"do not open the door while I am gone"*….

Me being grown, what did I do?

I always had a lot of mouth growing up, but this time I could not, did not open it.

I kept it all to myself, lived in the pain because I felt it was my fault for opening the door.

He said that he only wanted to use the phone, even as I spoke to him though the chain on the front door, I felt something wasn't right. The moment I closed the door to slide the chain across the slot and let it fall, I unchained another part of my young life.

As I lay there with my head facing the doorway to my room, with tears running down my face. I was fearful of my mom coming home, although naturally I would have been rescued, but my fear was that I opened the door when she was gone.

In fear as I looked out the window watching him leave.
In fear as I showed and cleaned myself.
In fear as I washed the sheets, and re-fixed my bed.
In fear because she said, "*do not open the door while I am gone*"...

In fear because I opened the door for him to use the phone that he didn't use.

Why was I in fear? Fear of a whooping? Fear of accused of lying? Fear for opening the door when I was not supposed to?

## In Jesus Name, Please Don't Touch Me There

Why am I speaking out? Because when you are molested or sexually assaulted, you live in darkness and do not say anything, it is like you are being violated all over again, naturally and spiritually. It's the same kind of fear that you had when their hand was covering your mouth or the finger is pointed in your face daring you to TELL what they did to you... You can be walking in fear, and not even realize it.

Although I am an adult, I still had to overcome fears from my childhood and teenage years, the fear of it happening again.

Sometimes something as simple as the way I answered or opened the door, what I wore to bed, the way I did dishes, doing dishes, my fear was not washing dishes, it was the position that I would wash them in. I washed dishes sideway, to "watch out" if anyone was sneaking up behind me.

One of my abusers use to come up behind me as I was doing dishes and inappropriately touch me, so I always lived in that fear even as an adult in my own home. Although I was in my own home with my husband and children, naturally nothing to fear, mentally doing...

"...Do not be scared or afraid, God will
protect you HE is always with you..."
**(Joshua 1:9)**

# MITZI L CARRASQUILLO

# PAIN ~ SHAME ~ and FEAR

*But those who wait on the Lord,*
*Shall renew their strength;*
*They shall mount up with wings like eagles,*
*They shall run and not be weary,*
*They shall walk and not faint.*
**(Isaiah 40:31)**

I hate when my mom's not home. Even at 16 when most teenage girls are battling with their mom, my mom and I have a relationship better than most of my friends and their mom have. She trusts in me and confides in me more than any of my other siblings.

I guess because I'm the oldest girl, and was the only girl until I was 12, when we formed this bond.

I hate dark, rainy, raw cold nights. It is such a reminder because of that awful night.

He was always staring at me or would feel my butt when I walk by him in the house. Sometimes he would come up behind me really close when I was doing the dishes. Or psst... psst... me when I walked by my mom's room on the way out the door, I'd think he wanted to ask me something, he'd pull the covers back and expose his naked body.

Whenever I told my mom; she said to just ignore him. At least everyone is home tonight, Mom should be here soon.

I don't know how long wakes take, but she shouldn't be long. She only went to support our neighbor, her friend whose brother passed away.

Plus everyone is home even one of my oldest brothers; he never bothers me when he's here.

I'll just stay in my room and go to bed, even though I wouldn't mind watching TV in the living room. *But he's in there.*

He knocked on my bedroom door and didn't wait to hear "come in"...

> *"...God is my refuge and strength,*
> *an ever- present help in trouble...."*
> **(Psalm 46:1)**

The next day at school I was numb, I went to the Guidance Counselor, and I told her everything, she listened intently, then asked have I told my mother, I said no, that I didn't know how.

The school officials called my mom to the school, and then the authorities were called.

# In Jesus Name, Please Don't Touch Me There

He was arrested; Department of Social Services came out to the house to file the report. My mother did not believe me, even before she said it, I knew it.

Just by the way she kept looking at me, especially when they informed her that he could not return to the home if I was there...

He left and stayed at a friend or relatives house for a few days.

Charges were filed against him, the day before we were to go to court my mother came and talked to me. She stated that this was not the first time that I accused someone of this, and asked why I lie so much?

What make me think everyone wants me? Because of her relationship with him, this was personal to her.

Sometimes on my way home from school I would see him leaving from the back of the house out the back door or sometimes he would drive by me and wave or smile at me, just spitefully to let me know that he had been at the house.

One day I came home from school, he was there in the house waiting to confront me. I was shocked, not to see him, but shocked that he was in the house. He asked one question; do you know what? I could go to jail for a long time with the lies you told?

There was no strength left in me, I thought I was going to pass out. I kept looking from her to him to her. Nothing could come out of mouth but tears down my face. As I looked at her for help, but there was none...

> "...She is clothed with strength and dignity;
> she can laugh, at the days to come..."
> **(Proverbs 31:25)**

The following day my mom took me to the court house to sign the release. I had never felt so weak, hurt, and bruised; she called the DSS worker and informed them of what happened. They stated that I still could not be in the home with him until their investigation is completed. If he returned to the home I could not be there, I would have to go to a foster, family or friend's home. My mom understood that it had to be me or him, and she knew that he was not going to leave.

One of my dearest friends at school was Dee Dee Woodbury; she knew what I was going through at home. Dee Dee was someone I could confide in, she understood me. We would do our homework together after school at her house, or I would stay for dinner, or just sit on her front porch. I loved to go to her home, it was always peaceful.

# In Jesus Name, Please Don't Touch Me There

It was just her… her lil' brother and Mom. Dee Dee had told her mom what was happening at my home, her mom allowed me to live with them.

Ms. Woodbury was a woman of Christ, always Praying. She welcomed me in her home, and was always sweet to me, as if I was another of her children.

Ms. Woodbury was always Praising God, I remember her first thing on Saturday morning playing her music, worshiping while cleaning.

I still remember her sitting with us talking about God, and Dee Dee and I would be rolling our eyes, trying to hold our laugh in.

Miss Woodbury always prayed for my mom, and our situation. Sometimes at night, I would hear her praying for my family before she went to bed.

Miss Woodbury was one of my first experiences of a God fearing woman of strength.

*"…The Lord is my strength and song,*
*And He has become my salvation…"*
**(Psalm 118:14)**

I was extremely shameful of what happened to me. I felt everyone in the neighborhood knew. Not only what happened, but also knew my mom's decision to have me live with Ms. Woodbury.

> *"I sought the Lord, and he answered me;*
> *he delivered me from all my fears.*
> *Those who look to him are radiant;*
> *their faces are never covered with shame."*
> **(Psalm 34:4-5)**

Not until years later did I understand that my mother made the best decision that she could have made at the time.

Because of the domestic abuse she suffered, I understood that the decision she made was out of fear for both of us. Her sending me to live with Ms. Woodbury was her way of protecting me.

> *"...Instead of their shame my people will receive*
> *a double portion, and instead of*
> *disgrace they will rejoice in their*
> *inheritance; and so they will inherit a*
> *double portion in their land, and*
> *everlasting joy will be theirs..."*
> **(Isaiah 61:7)**

# A FATHER OF THE FATHERLESS

God Bless Miss Woodbury, but what I wanted and felt what I needed the most in my life was my father.

Uncle Doug, my mom's eldest brother was the "father" who never missed a birthday, Valentines Day, Christmas, school plays, rewards for good report cards, and just constant hugs and kisses when he visited. When I was about 11 he moved away to Arizona. It was the saddest day for me. As I got older I never had a man teach me the value of a woman, how to be treated, and what to expect of a man. I spent so many years searching for and trying to understand that. The only thing that I knew was that he had to be like my Uncle Doug.

Although I my favorite uncle assumed the fatherly role, there was still a desire for my biological father.

> "...*I will never leave you*
> *nor forsake you*...."
> **(Hebrews 13:5)**

I met my dad when I was 16, my first time seeing him since I was 4 (*which I do not remember*). So this was technically my first time.

I can still remember the evening he came to Boston; we just

stood in the door way, not sure if my mom wanted him to come in. She then gave the approval for him to come into the reception hall, and then we sat in my bedroom.

Prior to this day, our communication had only been via letters, many letters.

I just stared at him at first, looking at all his features, trying to see what I had like him. It was like looking into a face of a stranger that you just happen to look like.

We were the same dark complexion, the darkness that caused me to be teased calling spook juice, Kizzy, or Blackie as a child.

We had the same big lips and brown eyes, with darkness under them. The same huge nostrils that my brothers teased me about, the same teeth, my reason for braces. My friends always teased me about my flat finger nails, and sometimes my mom would say you have fingers just like your dad.

Naturally, I had many features like him. We even have some of the same characteristics, our neatness and love of writing. I laugh sometimes, wondering did he love to write or was it because of his incarceration that he loved it?

Although we met, continued to write letters back and forth,

and I visited him while he was incarcerated.

I still had that incompleteness and emptiness of a father/daughter relationship in my life.

That incompleteness and emptiness became more prevalent on November 9, 1993. Suffering from schizophrenia, my father left home for a doctor's appointment, a suicide note was found in his bedroom, in which his body has never been found.

> *"...A father of the fatherless..."*
> **(Psalm 68:5)**

# MITZI L CARRASQUILLO

## ═══ WHAT I FEARED THE MOST ═══

The loss of my Dad added another layer of pain on me, another item on my list...

The counseling that I received at the age of 16 was nothing to assist me in what I would need to overcome as an adult.

There was not enough counseling in the world to help me with my Dad's loss, Sexual Abuse, Rape, Abandonment, Anger, Pain, Shame and Hurt.

Because I just continued to live with the pain for so many years, just continuing to push it down further and further inside of me, what I buried, rose up ready to explode December 1994.

> *"...What I feared has come upon me;*
> *what I dreaded has*
> *happened to me..."*
> **(Job 3:25)**

The last thing that I would ever want to happen, the one thing that I vowed would never happen, the one thing that I commended myself as parent, that I protected my daughters from...

What I feared the most, happened to my 4 year old daughter by a trusted family member. Someone I (as my mother did) would never suspect someone I truly love.

As I vacuumed my bedroom, I can still hear my daughter trying to talk to me over the vacuum cleaner. Her little voice was no comparison to the vacuum cleaner. Once I turned the vacuum off to hear what she was saying, she was still yelling as if the vacuum was still running. I swung around with such shock, anger and confusion (hoping that I didn't hear what I thought I heard) on my face that she took off running to her room. I ran after, grabbed and caressed her in my arms as I assured her that she did nothing wrong, she was a good girl, a big girl for telling me.

My first thought was to go find him and kill him, but I knew that I had to take care of her first. I made all the necessary phone calls, the police, ambulance, my husband at work, and sister in law.

I caressed her ponytails, and kissed her forehead as she told her story at the hospital, then the police station with such courage and in great detail. She had always been an intelligent little girl.

As my husband and I sat in the police station, all we thought about was the butcher knife under the driver's seat of our car parked in the lot of the station.

After taking all the necessary information, the police man walked us to the car assuring us that everything will work out, that we'll be ok, little did they know we left the police station driving for hours that night with her sleep in the backseat, while we were "praying" to find him.

Going through two court trials, pregnant with another child, feeling guilty and a failure as a parent, I became that victim all over again. I blamed myself, felt as if I failed her as a mother, and did not protect her. My only way to "protect" her was to over protect her.

While trying to be strong for her, all I did was add another layer to the junk I already had.

> *"...Jesus said, "The thief comes to*
> *steal, kill, and destroy; I have come*
> *that they may have life, and*
> *have it to the full..."*
> **(John 10:10)**

# MITZI L CARRASQUILLO

## ═══ LABORERS IN THE FIELD ═══

Prior to me accepting Jesus as my Lord and Savior, God always had me at the forefront of his thinking.

HE sent me just what I needed during this awful time. I remember during the two court trials, the family and therapy sessions, my neighbor Miss Sheila was known in the cul-de-sac as the "church lady", she was always putting scriptures in everyone's mailboxes or screen door, including mine.

> *"...Jesus said, "The harvest is plentiful,*
> *but the workers are few.*
> *Ask the Lord of the harvest, therefore*
> *to send out workers into his harvest field..."*
> **(Luke 10:2)**

She would invite me to her church, Boston Church of Christ, or to a Women's meeting, or a bible study group that she attended. And usually I would always politely say "no thanks".

Then once I accepted her offer and attended her church, went to a Women's meeting with her, and then started going to bible study at another church member's home, Miss Virginia.

Miss Virginia and her husband were the leaders of the bible study group. The bible study usually lasted about an hour or so.

Once the group ended at night, Miss Virginia would ask me to stay for a few minutes, and she and Miss Sheila would personally minister the plan God had for my life once I accepted Jesus as my Lord as Savior.

I can still hear Miss Virginia ministering to me at her beautiful cherry wood dining room table on why I needed to accept Jesus as my Lord and Savior. I would bang my fist and cry that I can't and I won't, and how it wasn't fair, that I will hate our abusers for the rest of my life.

She would minister to me the power of forgiveness, and how as long as I continued to hold on to the hate, anger and bitterness, I was only hurting myself, and in order for me to move forward I had to forgive.

Eventually I completely stopped going to the church, women's meetings, and the bible study. They would even come to my home, and I have to admit I would peep out the window, see it was them, ignore the doorbell, check the caller id when they called and did not answer the phone when they called, or made excuses. Soon they stopped "harassing" me, which was fine with me.

It was easier to be done with them than forgive. Unbeknownst to me all I did was go from having an unforgiving heart to Depression.

> *"...Bless them that curse you,*
> *and pray for them which*
> *despitefully use you..."*
> **(Luke 6:28)**

---

**Depression is a sickness that attacks everything that God has given you – Spirit, Soul, and Body**

- The first attack is of the Spirit/Mind (Mentally) - to isolate you, to get you thinking differently, negatively, and have a failure mentality....

- The second attack is the Soul (Emotionally) – thinking and feeling there is no way out, that death is the only escape...

- The third attack is the Body (Physically) – weakness, panic attacks, headaches, weight loss/gain, hair loss, heart palpitations, spirit of heaviness...

> *"...May God himself, the God of peace,*
> *Sanctify you through and through.,*
> *May your whole spirit, soul and body*
> *Be kept blameless at the coming..."*
> **(I Thessalonians 5:23)**

---

# MITZI L CARRASQUILLO

# ═══ DEPRESSION ~ "The Silent Killer" ═══

Never had I connected the Depression that I suffered from as an adult were effects linked directly from my childhood, the loss of my Dad, and my daughter's abuse. Those years of burying everything were the seeds planted for Depression to manifest.

I did not know how to heal from depression. At first I did not even realize that I was depressed, I thought I was just feeling bad. Depression makes you feel like there is nothing to live for, no life left; it is what I like to call *"the silent killer"*.

> *"...For God has not given us the spirit of fear;*
> *but of power, and of love,*
> *and of a sound mind..."*
> **(II Timothy 1:7)**

Depression had completely affected my entire life, at home, at work, and with friends.

From 1998 to 2001 I worked at Boston University in the Payroll Department, every morning when I arrived; I would look for a parking space way in the corner of the garage so no one could see me, it was a set plan each day on my hour lunch break.

I would go to my car to pray and cry for 45 minutes, and then go to a bathroom wash my face and head back to work like nothing happened.

Once I went for a yearly exam with my doctor and he began to ask me questions.

I just broke down in tears telling him all the things that were going on with me; I practically told him my life story. I opened up to him more that I did anyone else, even my husband. He listened so intently, and then asked if I would like to speak with someone else. I agreed. He referred me to a therapist that I visited about two times. I don't know why, but I always felt worse when I left their office. The one recommendation was always medications, in which I refused, another way of me having control over and thinking I can self heal.

Once I requested a copy of my medical records, and written was, "this patient is severely depressed and refuses medication".

> *"…I was in so much pain*
> *and felt no one*
> *could help me but God…"*
> **(Psalm 77:2)**

Sleep became my next meaning of a cure. I loved to sleep!

# In Jesus Name, Please Don't Touch Me There

On weekends I would sleep all day, wake up in the middle of the night and just cry, bawl out. Sleep to me was enjoyable because I was alone. The isolation, not wanting to be bothered with anyone, is another symptom of depression. I didn't want anyone's help, and would not let anyone in.

But I knew that I had to do something, anything to get over feeling like this.

Dodging my "church ladies" (running from my Jesus), refusing any assistance, keeping quiet and everything bottled up inside, I could and did not heal.

I began to suffer from terrible panic attacks, at first it was once or twice a week.

Then it became almost every night, so much that I would prepare myself at night for one, I would make sure that I had a glass of water at the nightstand.

And sure enough, like clockwork each night, there was my husband assisting me.

He would always say, what's the matter with you? Even him I did not share my depression with. I knew I needed something, but what?

Prior to my dad committing suicide in 1993, he gave me an old dark brown, soft cover, King James Bible that his Grandmother gave to him; I never wanted to use it. I treated it like an heirloom, it was very old, and I kept it on my dresser in the right hand corner for decoration I guess because I never used it.

Inside there were hand written notes and letters that my great grandmother had written to my Dad while he was incarcerated (*he was incarcerated the majority of my life*).

The thin yellow papers were so old and delicate; I placed them in a sandwich bag, and continued to keep them in the Bible.

My dad had even wrote a note to me as he passed it on, it said "Mitzi Darling, I am giving this to you, it's from your great grandmother, I was going to give it to Reggie (I know he needs it more than you) but I know you'll take care of it more than he would."

My dad could not have been more wrong; Dad, Reggie (*my oldest brother*), and I needed it.

What I began to do at night to "help" me overcome my panic attacks was sleep with that old Bible under my pillow. Although I had a stiff neck some days, but internally I began to feel better about myself and my panic attacks were not as frequent as they were.

# In Jesus Name, Please Don't Touch Me There

*"...By Jesus' stripes*
*I am healed..."*
**(1 Peter 2:24)**

═══════════════════════

Dr. Creflo Dollar's definition of pain, "Pain is a highly concentrated thought."

# MITZI L CARRASQUILLO

## GOD, THE FIRST, ONLY and LAST MAN

GOD, the First, Only, and Last "Man" to EVER LOVE YOU! Up until April 7, 2001 I felt I had nothing to live for. Not knowing who I was, or feeling loved, I was looking for a quick and easy way out, just like my Dad.

Praise God for my Heavenly Father who lets me know who I am as His daughter! In HIS Word HE tells me what HE thinks of me and most of all how much he loves me. It took nearly 35 years for me to realize that God loves me. HE loves me unconditionally! I've been made whole and complete in HIM. HE is the father that I can always depend on.

When you have so much that happen to you, it's very hard to believe that God loves you. I always wondered, why He would allow these things to happen, if He loves me?

If he loves me, why was I abused, why did I get a whooping for telling the truth? What form of love is that? Did I do something wrong and this is His way of punishing me? Why was my daughter abused?

It is NOT God's fault! He Loves You! God would never allow

or do anything to hurt or harm you in anyway. I know it may seem like HE is the one to blame.

HE would not hurt something that he created. GOD Loves You!

> *"...For God so loved the world that*
> *He gave His only begotten Son,*
> *that whoever believes in Him*
> *should not perish but*
> *have everlasting life..."*
> **(John 3:16)**

Just as we love our children, and want the best for them, HE gave his "best", so you can be and have the best!

It has been a Blessing to know that God created me (and you) for a reason. A reason that I now know, and I Pray that you will come to know also. Who would harm someone that he created? You were not created by accident. *God loving me taught me how to love and forgive others...*

> *"...Before I formed you in the womb*
> *I knew you; and before you came forth,*
> *I sanctified you, and I ordained you*
> *a prophet..."*
> **(Jeremiah 1:5)**

# FORGIVENESS, IS IT POSSIBLE?

*Forgiveness is it possible?* I have to admit this was the first and hardest thing for me to do, but it was the *best thing that I've ever done.*

Forgiving was hard because, my idea of forgiving was as if I was letting "them" get one up on me, you know like I was a punk.

When you have an eye for an eye attitude, you don't get mad... you get even. Forgiving is almost impossible. You feel as though you lost the fight, they got away.

> *"...Do not repay evil*
> *for evil..."*
> **(Proverbs 20:22)**

It's so easy to hate the person, not only is it easy but it's natural, and it actually feels good. I had a serious hate for my offenders and my daughters that I had to get rid of. I had to learn to hate the sin, not the person.

> *"...Wicked people will not make*
> *righteous decisions ..."*
> **(Proverbs 29:2)**

Holding onto the hate, anger, bitterness, not only made me sick, I gained weight, my hair fell out, I distanced myself, I was always mad, I did not love myself, and guess what?, I didn't love anyone else neither. I had so many years of hate embedded inside of me that I did not know where to start or who to forgive first. But what I did know was that I had to release this, because although I didn't take my life that fateful day, any day my life could be taken with what I was carrying around in me. Those I hated life would have been spared, not mine…

*"…How do you take all the pain*
*and go on? Walk in the*
*Love of God…"*
**(1Corinthians 13:4-8)**

---

Until you forgive, you cannot go forward, sideward, or upwards. ONLY BACKWARDS or DOWNWARDS-your past will always be your Present and Future…

Unforgiveness keeps you from living your life to the full potential.

*You are withholding your Healing Manifestation; you cannot Heal until you Forgive.*

# THE LORD IS A HEALER

There were layers (shame, guilt, fear, unloved, and unforgiveness) that God removed to place me where I am now. Many have been by faith. It is not easy; my overcoming of sexual abuse, rape, and depression was a process.

As you read, I tried to "heal" myself from shame by isolating and putting up a brick wall, I tried to "heal" myself from guilt by unforgiveness, I tried to "heal" myself from fear, doing dishes sideways, overprotecting my daughter, I tried to "heal" myself from panic attacks, assuring that I had a glass of water available, I tried to "heal" myself from depression, sleeping with a Bible under my pillow, for my panic attacks – these were all my "healing mechanisms".

*"...The Lord is my Healer..."*
**(Exodus 15:26)**

Not until I accepted Jesus as my Lord and Savior, believed and received what HE said concerning healing was I able to heal.

There was only one "man" who was able to help me, not my father, doctor, therapists, or my husband.

*"...He sent forth his word
and healed them; he rescued
them from the grave..."*
**(Psalm 107:20)**

What I have also learned from my healing process is to also pray for those who abused (you) me. In most cases abusers are victims also, who also need healing. I Pray that they will never harm another individual, and that they be healed of their sickness.

*"...Pray for those who
hurt you..."*
**(Matthew 5:44)**

Sexual abuse, rape is a sickness; they (the abusers) are lacking something in their life. It is an act of anger, rage, and power.

Because molestation/rape is usually done by a family member, you also need to pray for the curse to be broken, in most families Sexual molestation/rape is a generational curse.

Praise God for his Mighty Work! God's wonderful Healing power has given me the strength to pray with and for my abusers, as well as my daughters.

I've attended and sat at some of the same family gatherings

# In Jesus Name, Please Don't Touch Me There

and dinner tables with our abusers.

Just imagine, the love of God made it possible that the same men that I truly hated, despised of, drove around looking for with a knife under the seat to kill, I can now hold their hand in Prayer.

Praise God! Some are now my brothers in Christ! Amen!

*As long as you continue to meditate on the Word of God, the love of God, your pain will diminish and your healing will manifest.*

*Jesus said: "...Love the Lord your God with all your heart and with all your soul and with all your mind.*
*"... This is first and greatest commandment. And the second is like it..."*
*"...Love your neighbor as yourself..."*
**(Matthew 22:37-39)**

# MITZI L CARRASQUILLO

# MEDITATING ON THE WORD
# OF GOD BRINGS GREAT SUCCESS

*Meditating on the Word of God Brings Great Success.* Meditating on words not of God is what caused me to worry, unable to overcome fear, caused panic attacks, and depression.

> *"...This is my comfort and consolation*
> *in my affliction; that your word has*
> *revived me and given me life..."*
> **(Psalm 119:50)** (Amplified Bible)

The effects of my childhood (and what happened to my daughter) that led to my depression as an adult has what I call *"trigger moments"* moments when you reflect on the past or hurt. There were things that remind me of my past, sometimes something as simple as the weather. Rainy, raw, cold days use to cause me to feel weak and weary. Those are the days when I want to crawl in the bed and "meditate" with my Lauryn or Dru Hill CD, their music use to be my source of meditation that only made me feel worse. Yep me, Lauryn, Dru, a box of tissues, tears of pain, but I still felt the same way. Those are the days that I have to pray without ceasing, don't imagine or dwell on those old thoughts.

*"...Establish a relationship
with Him..."*
**(Isaiah 26:3)**

There is nothing like meditating in the Word of God.

Meditating in the Word of God is like getting yourself dolled up from the inside out. You know how you like to look good on the outside; get your hair, nails, and eyebrows done, with a nice new outfit and shoes to match, including accessories and makeup? Just like you do all of this so that your "outer body" is beautiful and presentable, you have to do this to your inner body as well. To get your inner body dolled up, you need to fill it with love, joy, peace, kindness, long suffering, kindness, goodness, faithfulness, gentleness, and self control. I had to change the mental picture, my inner image to the image that God created me.

*"...I will meditate on all your works
and consider all
your mighty deeds..."*
**(Psalm 77:12)**

Get alone with God to talk to Him regarding what you are going through, regardless of what it is. Plan to have quiet time to hear directly from Him regarding your situation, there is nothing God can't do.

I keep scriptures on my refrigerator, in my car, at work, in my wallet, but the most important place is in my heart and in my mouth.

> *"...Your word is a lamp to my feet*
> *and a light for my path..."*
> **(Psalm 119:105)**

I've replaced Lauryn and Dru with Pastor Kitt's "None Like You". There are still tissues, but they now are for a different purpose, tears of joy! Amen!

*Do not be afraid to talk to God, HE will be with you and give you the Strength with each step you take*

# MITZI L CARRASQUILLO

# ═ STRENGTH, THE PIECE OF CLOTHING ═
# THAT DID NOT "FIT" ME

*Strength was the piece of clothing that did not "fit "me.* Strength was a characteristic that I had to grow into to (*and continuing to grow in*), which started when I begin to know who I was in Christ.

I felt as if I was the weakest woman on the face of the earth, on the outside you probably would not have known on the outside, but inside I was that 6 year old again. I felt that I had no voice, no power to do anything, and failed at everything, even protecting my own child. Weakness was prevalent in my life; I could not help myself without Him.

> *"...Trust in the Lord with all your heart*
> *and lean not on your own understanding;*
> *in all your ways acknowledge him,*
> *and he will make your paths straight..."*
> **(Proverbs 3:5-6)**

Allowing God to be my strength, I first had to understand Him, build confidence in Him, and Trust in His Word.

> *"...The Word of God*
> *Is always the truth..."*
> **(John 17:17)**

Because I lacked confidence and trust in people, having confidence in God was a huge step for me, I needed to have confidence in Him in order for me to trust him.

> *"...God is not a man, that he should lie,*
> *nor a son of man, that he should*
> *change his mind..."*
> **(Numbers 23:19)**

As I begin to cultivate my relationship with God I had to change the way I saw myself and know that I could not do it on my own. God had to be my strength to conquer fear, to defeat, and overcome any circumstances. The things that happened to me opened a door for me to be an over comer.

> *"...Finally be strong in the Lord*
> *and His mighty power..."*
> **(Ephesians 6:10)**

Sexual abuse has a way of making you feel unworthy, useless and unclean. The repair starts inside out...

What I was trying to do is repair from the outside in by living a life of pretence, trusting no one around myself or my children, keeping a wall or a shield up when meeting someone. I stayed private and did not let anyone "inside "my feelings.

# In Jesus Name, Please Don't Touch Me There

*Faith in the Word of God taught me how to change my walk from with my head down, to making eye contact, and smiling from the inside out.*

> "...And be not conformed to this world,
> but be ye transformed by the renewing
> of your minds so that you may prove
> the more excellent way!..."
> **(Romans 12:2)**

# MITZI L CARRASQUILLO

# ═══ FAITH IN GOD IS WHAT HAS ═══ SUSTAINED ME

*Faith in God is what sustained and created me to be the person I am today...*

My trust, belief and faith in people, especially men were taken from me. I didn't have faith in myself, it was hard to have faith for something and you look around and see nothing. By faith, I had to learn to have faith...

I had to have faith in the Word of God, coming from Dr. Creflo Dollar on April 7, 2001 as I crawled on my knees out of the closet. I had faith that day, unbeknownst to me. I didn't know what to expect, but I knew that it could not get any worse than it was.

> *"...Faith comes by hearing and hearing by the Word of God..."*
> **(Romans 10:17)**

Its funny how life works, my bedroom closet is such a symbol to me now. As young as 9 years old I could still remember whenever I was hurt or upset I would go in my bedroom closet. The closet back then was a safe haven for me.

I would sit on my shoes; keep the door cracked ever so gently to let a little light in, because I was scared of the dark. No one ever knew I was in there, at least I thought until one day my mom caught me leaving the closet, and said, girl what are you doing in there?

I would make up some story that I was looking for something.

> *"...Now faith is being sure of*
> *what we hope for and certain*
> *of what we do not see..."*
> **(Hebrews 11:1)**

As I got older in my teenage years I would do my writing in there or just stand with my back against the wall, eyes closed, praying. I had faith when I didn't know that I had. The reason that I say this is because I always thought it couldn't get any worse. In order for me to think that it couldn't get any worse, I had to believe something else, that it could get better, be better, regardless of the "worse" that I was looking at.

> *"...And without Faith it is impossible*
> *to please God, because anyone*
> *who comes to him must believe that*
> *he exists and that he rewards those*
> *who earnestly seek him..."*
> **(Hebrews 11:6)**

# ═══ PURPOSE ═══

*April 8, 2001, when I accepted Jesus as my Lord and Savior, was a confirmed validation of the plan that God had for my life...*

Being the daughter of a dad who suffered schizophrenia and a mom who also suffered from depression, driving my car off of the Tobin Bridge probably would not be a surprise to anyone. The enemy had a plan, and I was standing in agreement with him. But guess what? God's plan was bigger.

> *"...There is no wisdom, no insight,*
> *no plan that can succeed*
> *against the Lord..."*
> **(Proverbs 21:30)**

I am a walking testimony of what "The Word of God" can do with your life, when you think that you have no "life" left. Regardless of all that I have been through in my 41 years, I know that I am here for a purpose to be fulfilled for Jesus Christ.

I write this book not only as a survivor, but also as a Mother of a survivor of sexual abuse.

I was in no position to spiritually, mentally, or emotionally

Had I not forgave our abusers, this would not have been possible.

If I found her abuser that fateful night, this book would have been written from Framingham State Prison (the women's prison in Boston). This story and format would have been totally different, not glorifying God for receiving his Salvation, his love as a parent, the power to forgive, to heal, to strengthen, and the faith to overcome.

> *"...In the same way, let your light shine*
> *before men that they may see*
> *your good deed and praise*
> *your Father in heaven..."*
> **(Matthew 5:16)**

Many things may have happened to you, but that does not change who you are and who God called you to be.

Whatever your Testimony is, know that God Loves You, learn to Forgive so you can Heal. You no longer have to be in Fear, because the Strength of the Lord is upon you. While you Meditate on HIS Word, may you have mighty Faith to do all things, and the Joy of the Lord will keep you in perfect Peace, that you will come to know Who You Are, and the Purpose and Plan for your Life.

Salvation is the key to your new life, and always Acknowledge

**In Jesus Name, Please Don't Touch Me There**

HIM that gave you Life, HE IS THE AUTHOR for all you do.

*"...God's Love will cause you to overcome.*
*You are more than a conqueror*
*through Jesus..."*
**(Romans 8:37)**

━━━━━━━━━━━━━━━━━

# MITZI L CARRASQUILLO

## TOO YOUNG

*I was too young,*
*too young to remember clearly*
*It was too chaotic,*
*too chaotic for a 4-year old*
*I was too oblivious,*
*too oblivious to comprehend what was happening*
*It was too blurry,*
*too blurry to recall something I worked so hard to forget*
*I had too much pressure,*
*too much pressure to relive an unwanted past*
*It was too easy,*
*too easy to give my all to the Lord in return for my pain*
*I was too young,*
*too young to remember clearly*

\*\*My innocence was ripped from beneath me when I was sexually abused at the tender age of 4, and held onto the pain unknowingly until August 8, 2001, when I dedicated my life unto the Lord. It's been a rocky road so far and I know there will be more speed bumps to come. But with Him

> *"...all things are possible*
> *If you believe..."*
> **(Mark 9: 23)**

*Jazmine Carrasquillo* ~ age 16

*My Past will Prosper my future...*
*Mitzi L. Carrasquillo*

# MITZI L CARRASQUILLO

## PRAYER OF SALVATION

The primary purpose of Prayer is to seek Him. God will reward those who diligently seek him. My greatest reward that I have received was for God to give himself to me, He has been my restorer.

When I look back at my life God was always there, even when I thought He wasn't or could care if He was. I use to think that I didn't need God, one day my girlfriend Jeannette was ministering to me, and my foolish self said "I got this, God don't work fast enough for me"… What a fool I was!

On April 7, 2001, the moment that I said those 3 little words while sitting in my bedroom closet with my knees in my chest and head between my legs, contemplating the quickest way to take my life, I opened the door and gave God permission to invade my life. I could not help myself without him. That day I gave HIM permission to get involved, and seek his assistance.

When I accepted him as my Lord and Savior it was like a level of weight was lifted off of me, or like I could now move forward. I always used the analogy of a huge green garbage bag filled with bricks, that each had their own name, depressed, overweight, low self esteem, hate, anger, bitterness, ugly, loser, sad, loss of a father, etc.

## PRAYER OF SALVATION (cont'd)

My bag was so full, I couldn't take a step forward, I was just still, and it was weighing me down.

Are you ready to empty your bag?

There aren't enough words to explain the Peace **(John 14:27)** and Joy **(Psalm 28:7)** that I received accepting Jesus as my Lord & Savior.

So I ask the question: Are you going are you going to turn the light switch to the right and stay in that dark place? Or will you turn it to the left, the beautiful and full light?

Accepting Jesus as your Lord and Savior is just making this simple prayer. I guarantee your life will never be the same! God has come to give you life, a new life!

## Salvation Prayer

If you do not know Jesus as your Lord and Savior, simply pray the following prayer in faith and Jesus will be your Lord!

Heavenly Father I come to you in the name of Jesus. Your word says,

*"...Whosoever shall call on the name of the Lord*
*shall be saved and If thou shalt confess with thy mouth*
*the Lord Jesus, and shalt believe in thine heart*
*that God hath raised him from the dead,*
*thou shalt be saved..."*
**(Acts 2:21; Romans 10:9)**

I take you at your word. I confess that Jesus is Lord. And I believe in my heart that you raised him from the dead. Thank you for coming into my heart, and for being Lord over my life. I am now a child of God. Amen

If you prayed this Prayer, I would love to hear from you. Please write and tell me about it. I want to send you something to start your new life.

P.O. Box 2474
Germantown, Maryland 20875-2474
proverbs03125@yahoo.com

# MITZI L CARRASQUILLO

# In Jesus Name, Please Don't Touch Me There

*"... and you have been given fullness in Christ,
who is the head over every
power and authority..."*
**(Colossians 2:10)**

**About The Author**

Mitzi has been married to her wonderful husband Jose for 20 years. They have three beautiful children, daughters, Jeanee 19, Jazmine 16, and son, Jose III, 11 years old.

The Carrasquillo's attend Victory Christian Church International in Gaithersburg, Maryland under the guidance of Extraordinary Pastors Dwayne and Kitt Brewington. Mitzi serves as a Nursery Teacher with Infants in the Generation Changers Student Ministry.

The Carrasquillo's reside in Germantown, Maryland.

*"You are here to solve a problem for God. You already have the ability/grace to do whatever God called you to do"*

*Pastor Dwayne Brewington, Victory Christian Church International.*